Formation Groups

Transforming Disciples

A resource for small groups

ANDREW GOLDSMITH

ISBN: 1548217727
ISBN-13: 978-1548217723

DEDICATION

To all those who have invested in me, built me up, prayed for me and taught me in the faith, who have led to a deeper heart-and-head knowledge of the Son of God who loved me and gave himself for me. Especially to those in Long Crendon, Leeds, Ruislip, Corsham, Virginia and Ampthill – thank you.

CONTENTS

Chapter 1

Introduction

Called to Grow

Growing as a Christian is something every Christian experiences. As we look back, we can see signs of growth, even if unsteady, erratic or slow at times. It may be subtle or spectacular. Perhaps our 'growth chart' reminds us of the cautionary note attached to various financial products: 'past performance is not an indicator of future results'. Yet we only have to read the pages of the New Testament to find how clearly God has called us to a life of growth. He has also provided for it and encourages it. In Christ he promises it. This short book offers some encouragement and resources along the path to growth.

We are called to be disciples and make disciples. And we're called to grow. The principal means which the Bible points to is through God's Word preached and applied. This is why biblical preaching is so central to church life. The preaching provides the main source of teaching, exhortation, encouragement and spiritual food for the whole church, as the gathered and connected body. There are other ways to receive teaching, but this is how the Bible presents the primary and normative pattern for the whole church, for our growth and unity together. Just one reason why coming to church is important.

We can also expect that as we take in the Word, chew on it and digest its meaning alongside others, this growth will be seen not just in knowledge but also in confidence, love, wisdom and so on.

In looking at how this growth alongside other disciples is presented in scripture, a number of Bible texts offer profoundly significant encouragement to seek growth in Christ. This is a rich and varied theme throughout Old and New Testaments, so these examples are not an exhaustive account by a long stretch.

Jesus uses the everyday analogy of the vine (John, chapter 15), which would be growing on walls and homes throughout Israel. It was a vivid, recognizable image of growth, as Christ calls us to be connected to him life, drawing life from him, bearing fruit as we grow.

> "I am the vine; you are the branches. If a man remains in me and I in him, he will bear much fruit; apart from me you can do nothing. ... This is to my Father's glory, that you bear much fruit, showing yourselves to be my disciples" (John 15:5,8)

He clearly provides for growth, and expects it.

To the church in Colosse, Paul's letter lifts their sights from the distractions of non-gods and wrong-headed thinking of where their confidence was, and sets their minds on Christ. He longs for them to not just be confident but also maturing, growing:

> So then, just as you received Christ Jesus as Lord, continue to live in him, rooted and built up in him, strengthened in the faith as you were taught, and overflowing with thankfulness. (Colossians 2:6-7)

This is no flimsy, ramshackle growth but something secure, ongoing and brimming over into our attitudes and relationships.

To the church in Ephesus, when Paul depicts the various ministries of the church body (4:7-11), they all rely on sharing God's word and are intended for our growth. This word-ministry transformation comes especially through preaching and teaching, yet the description of this beautiful growth applies to disciples growing and being transformed together:

> ... to prepare God's people for works of service, so that the body of Christ may be built up until we all reach unity in the faith and in the knowledge of the Son of God and become mature, attaining to the whole measure of the fullness of Christ. (Ephesians 4:12-13)

This growth is certainly not limited to God working through those in recognized ministry roles – our pastors, preachers, leaders. Some are gifted and called in specific ways, and we can all recall the experiences of God using such gifts, yet this growth in Christ also comes through the Lord using 'one another', the body of Christ. So we find the exhortation:

> Therefore encourage one another and build each other up, just as in fact you are doing. (1 Thessalonians 5:11)

That certainly has a familiar, happy ring to it, and perhaps we can recall significant 'builders' in our lives as God works through those alongside us. It should not be a rare event, reserved for spiritual mountain tops, but found in the ordinary gathering, not least as the 'ordinary' church. The writer to the Hebrews picks up on the same theme, the expectation of being involved in each other's lives bringing growth, transformation, encouragement:

> … let us consider how we may spur one another on toward love and good deeds. Let us not give up meeting together, as some are in the habit of doing, but let us encourage one another—and all the more as you see the Day approaching. (Hebrews 10:24-25)

It is abundantly clear that to be a disciple of Christ is never intended to be a static 'status', as if it is simply a membership update to our spiritual CV or our online profile. It is meant to be a dynamic, transforming reality of growth in Christ. Discipleship involves ongoing maturity, growing in love and knowledge, putting off the old and putting on the new self, with character, faith and understanding working out in the everyday arenas of our relationships, workplace, priorities, prayer patterns and service of others.

The Lord provides for this and calls us for this, and we can engage in such discipleship in 'small, medium and large sizes'.

Discipleship: Small, Medium and Large?

Being gathered as a congregation under Bible preaching is vital to making disciples, to glue together the fellowship of the church, to shape and energize it in mission, to bind up the hurting and strengthen the weak, to speak into the life of the church as a whole. All this should be our expectation as we gather, and increasingly our experience as we come to church, open to God's speaking and leading.

However, the 'large' setting is typically not the most practical context for working out for ourselves the 'what next?' which might follow from the Bible's teaching. What are the practical implications for my Christian life at my workplace, in my marriage, with my financial priorities? How can I revive my struggling prayer life? These are everyday questions which matter to the Lord in our discipleship, with practical implications for ourselves. Yet during a sermon is generally an inconvenient time to raise personal questions *("would you just stop there a minute?*

How does this apply to raising my teenager?", "Can you suggest how I bring this into my sales team meeting tomorrow?", "I agree, but I'm really struggling to live by that truth right now.", and so on).

And it's not just the 'Christian life' questions, but also the opportunity to go deeper in studying and discussing the Bible and its message more broadly. Perhaps we hope for a forum to encourage one another in how we respond to the message in everyday life. This can be *indicated* by a sermon, but discussion and follow-up aren't easy there and then. Yet these practical applications from the preaching are vital in being and making disciples. These are at the heart of what small groups should include.

Small groups can be ***so*** helpful. Many a thriving church, across the world in diverse church settings from modern American mega-churches to small, rural churches in central Africa or Asia have found the small group the place to take those questions, that Bible-searching and the life-sharing into a more flexible and intimate context. Whether they are called house groups, small groups, life groups or plain Bible study groups, the outcomes can be precious and life-changing indeed.

The strengths of small groups are in being a place for spiritual growth as we build up one another, through Bible study and discussion tailored to the group. There is the fellowship of a group smaller than the whole gathered church, with time for conversation, questions, sharing in prayer and meals, the tears and laughter, sharing concerns and giving encouragement. A small group can be a place to identify and explore spiritual gifts and ways of service, and simply making friends. Small groups can excel in these things. I have had over 20 years of sharing in small group life, most of that leading groups in various settings, and seen the way God brings growth, joy and transformation.

The Lord Jesus invested in his three closest friends, and the Twelve, and through their testimony changed the world. Small groups work.

> As iron sharpens iron, so one man sharpens another. (Proverbs 27:17)

We are meant to be alongside one another, rubbing off some corners, honing some edges, renewing and restoring as the Lord uses us. But … there are times when life gets in the way. Sometimes a different model, a still smaller group, is needed.

When life gets in the way

Jeff is an intensive care nurse, who works shifts including nights. Robert works in warehousing, also on a varied rota where one week's pattern is different from the next. Rachel is a care assistant in a nursing home, who loves her job and her church, but the 'funny hours' make attending any church group on a regular basis quite difficult. David is a successful sales manager, who travels the country visiting car dealerships and is away from home at least two nights a week. Tracy is a single mum, juggling a part-time job with school runs, after school clubs and wanting to be more connected to the church mid-week. Peter and Jackie have two young children, and elderly parents needing significant support. Graham and Penny are trying to remember who is on the 'taxi run' for their three teenagers with multiple commitments this week.

All of the above are fictional yet typical in many a church setting. Every church leader will recognize these – the people in your church family who would love to be part of a regular small group, meeting for Bible study, prayer and encouragement, but the idea of every second Tuesday evening, or perhaps *any* Tuesday evening, is out of the question. They (and we) miss out, unless a more flexible opportunity can be found.

If only several of these people could get together, whenever and wherever, regularly but on an *ad hoc* basis, and get into the Bible and share how they are doing in their walk with Jesus ...

When a small group is not small enough

Another frequent barrier to deeper engagement in discipleship is simply when the small group is not small enough.

Most small groups tend to be of a size where it is difficult to move towards deeper accountability with one another, to a wholehearted and frank openness about spiritual struggles and questions. It's clearly *desirable* to have discussions about our own Christian life and the nitty gritty of being a Christian in everyday life. In our best moments we can also approach this with a willingness to let others challenge and encourage. But it is hard to envisage this *practically,* with too many people in the group. Normal small groups (perhaps 8-12 people) are typically not geared up for this, and leaders may not feel equipped either. Some are, but these are exceptions in my experience. Such groups can be wonderful places for prayer and growth, but sharing with a dozen other people of varied age and backgrounds on our personal struggles would be daunting for many people. We can't expect to know everyone at a 'no holds barred' level of openness.

For such accountability, a safe space to grow and receive, an even smaller group is more realistic and helpful.

It is this level of authentic fellowship, the intimacy of Christian friendship and accountability in a deeper way that, when we have experienced it, we know we richly value and desire. A small group can be a great experience, but can fail to achieve a more accountable, personal engagement still, with God and with each other as disciples, by being too large or diverse, or focused mainly on Bible study for understanding without application. So how can we enable that change?

Fridge Rights

Someone once described this 'deeper engagement' with each other this way: who do you know well enough in your church that you'd readily invite them into your home and talk about anything in your hallway, or better still in your lounge, or better still at the family meal table? Who do you know well enough that they have 'fridge rights' – you'd welcome them in, at any time, and think nothing of them helping themselves to something from your fridge![1] You are close enough that they are like one of the family. That, perhaps, is an example of how we can expect to be closer or more open with one another spiritually.

I'm aware that for some in our churches this may be challenging, or an eye-opener that discipleship is meant to be like this. Yet surely it is meant to be like this. Many Christians have never experienced this kind of engagement with fellow Christians about living their faith, their discipleship. Many churches have not practically provided a forum for it.

Again, we shouldn't expect such accountability and this level of personal engagement with *everyone else* in church. But each of us should seek it and we all need it from *someone else*, with a few people perhaps, as part of what true Christian friendship and discipleship involves. It has the power to transform our lives in deep and significant

---

[1] I'm grateful to Major Mark Herbert (Salvation Army) for this cool idea.

ways as the Lord uses other disciples to build us up, to transform us through teaching, correction, nurture, encouragement and love. And we can be used to transform others, as God works through us too.

So what we are looking for, to help people grow as disciples, and especially those who need a more flexible, smaller and more intentional group, is a new form of small group.

And it is a suggestion along these lines that this short book offers and outlines – **Formation groups**.

Chapter 2

What are Formation groups?

Formation Groups - even smaller groups

The aim of a Formation group is to provide time together as a group of just four people, to foster a deliberate, intentional desire to grow as Christians, to be transforming disciples. With just four in the group, it enables a greater degree of authentic, deeper engagement with each other and time for all to share in significant ways.

A smaller group reduces the 'fear factor' compared to a larger group of perhaps ten or more in a typical church Bible study group. With just a few men or women, experiencing and encouraging deeper accountability, there is the freedom to ask one another questions, share doubts or struggles, challenge and prompt one another. It is not realistic to aim for this in a large group of mixed age, background, gender and maturity. Such a small group with clear aims will offer friendship and fellowship, with time for one another.

With such a small group, it also enables the *flexibility* many need, around busy lives and unpredictable or demanding schedules.

A Formation group will be four people of the same sex, who commit to meet together regularly to study the Bible, to discuss practical aspects of their Christian lives and to pray together, all with the aim of growing together in Christ.

A Formation group can also be offered for a short, defined time rather than indefinitely. We trialed this initiative, starting with six months as the initial commitment, but have found groups continuing well beyond this. We share some of our experience in the final chapter.

The aims

The goal is simply to be growing in Christ. How Formation groups enable this is with time together to foster a deliberate, intentional desire to grow as Christians, to be transforming disciples. They aim to provide a context with a greater degree of accountability than Sunday morning fellowship or a large Bible study house group permits. The openness and accountability stems from the Bible study and discussion questions, and simply getting to know a few friends well. This cultivates the freedom to ask one another questions, to share doubts or struggles with honesty and support, to challenge and prompt one another around matters of everyday life as a disciple.

It also aims to build genuinely deeper friendships, which will last beyond the group.

How long, how often?

We suggested that initially a Formation group would agree to meet once a month for six months. They might meet for an hour and a half to two hours each time. So it is not a big commitment in terms of time, and limited to six sessions in theory. Hopefully this makes it accessible for many. If a group wanted to continue, that may well be fine, but setting the six month limit gives individuals the opportunity to either return to another group or ministry area, or take a break before setting up a new group with others who have not yet experienced it. In our experience, word will tend to spread and others will want to become part of a Formation group.

In practice, the first six Bible study sessions have taken longer than six months to complete for most groups, as they have also deliberately taken time to meet socially – a meal, with family, a Saturday morning coffee - or simply for prayer, before returning to the 'programme'.

The content

Each session would aim to include Bible study, discussion, prayer, and feedback from earlier sessions. The **Bible study** would either take a book (e.g. Philippians) or could follow a series of Bible texts on a theme, but in each case the aim is to gain understanding and promptly move to personal application – to generate discussion of how this impacts your Christian life, your walk with God, your vitality and growth as a disciple of Jesus. Chapters 4-6 provide three sets of Bible studies: on Philippians, the Psalms, and John's Gospel chapters 13-16.

The **discussion time** would have a set topic to generate opportunities to share and encourage one another. These would aim to be practical matters, the stuff of everyday discipleship, such as 'my relationship to Jesus', 'prayer life', 'spiritual growth and battles', 'money, work, stewarding my time', 'relationships and family', 'godly goals and service'. Chapter 7 provides examples, with a range of six such topics and suggested starter questions. In practice a group can adapt to their own needs.

The **prayer time** would be to pray for one another specifically, to build up and encourage. There would also be value in short **feedback**: how are things going since we last met, talked and prayed?

An example of how this might work in a mid-week evening is as follows: e.g. 10 minutes for chat and catching up as the kettle boils and hard decisions are made over which biscuits to open; 30-40 minutes for Bible study and discussion around the text; 40 minutes discussion time on a discipleship topic, 20 minutes prayer, 10 minutes feedback and booking the next meeting date. Around 2 hours of great investment, of iron sharpening iron.

These timings are all flexible of course. Each group has a different dynamic, different venues, different personalities. Over time, Bible study and discussion may well grow in duration and depth. But the core 'menu', the content, will be consistent and kept in focus. The group meets for transformation and growth, not just for a catch-up over coffee.

What about regular small groups and prayer triplets?

The Formation groups are not intended to replace these, but bring something new and different, with quite different aims and expectations. Small groups are a vital part of my home church and many others like us. Their life and ministry around Bible study, prayer and fellowship should be encouraged. Prayer triplets may already be going on in your fellowship too, and indeed deliver what Formation groups aim to achieve. They may wish to use these ideas and Bible studies themselves. However, for those needing something smaller or more flexible, or a more intentional group, or having struggled for other reasons to find a group to regularly commit to, Formation groups may well offer a timely and effective option.

What now?

If you find the needs of your church fellowship are reflected in what has been outlined, then perhaps it is worth investigating or running Formation groups for yourself.

Within our local church, the need was very clear, and I suspect we are not that unusual. Certainly the aim of deeper discipleship and transforming growth needed no discussion at all! So … on to the launch platform.

Chapter 3

Getting started

Leadership and oversight

A vital part to any new initiative in churches, alongside prayerful planning and clear communication, is capable leadership. The leader of a Formation group needs to have sufficient spiritual maturity to support and guide others, and a suitable level of pastoral wisdom and sensitivity. They may well have led small groups in some other way in the past. But the role is different from a Bible study leader of a small group in that the Bible study element of a Formation group is weighted more to intentional application than is often the case. In a group of just four people it is also clearly a more collaborative exercise – there is much more time and opportunity for all to contribute. The leader is as much a facilitator of the study as the teacher.

However, each group needs a leader, not least as a means of organizing and communicating, and the all-important but elusive task of getting that next date in the diary.

In our case, I approached eight people not currently leading existing small groups, and none of them in a small group, but with the qualities needed to lead. We did not want to impact our ongoing and healthy small group network by taking from that set of leaders. It is also an opportunity to grow leadership skills in others.

Initial direction and support were provided along with all the materials needed to begin (which are available in the following chapters). Regular pastoral support, input and advice was also offered, especially as new groups got off the ground and new people joined in.

Recruiting a group

This is clearly a very important step. In terms of the people, the first people in mind were those not already supported by others, i.e. those not currently connected in a church small group network or in prayer triplets. Formation groups were to offer a range of new, flexible groups with intentional discussions and met a clear need, but they were not developed and introduced whilst also dismantling existing groups or other effective areas of discipleship ministry. So careful pastoral thought needs to be given at this starting point, of who to recruit and to invite.

It may be helpful to ask the group leaders to consider who they might approach, based on who they know and perhaps at least one person they are concerned for. This looks out across a congregation and asks the question, 'who struggles to be connected?' The church leaders can offer help at this point. Then it's time to pray and begin to invite people, explaining what the group would involve.

Signing up - agreeing the goals

Each group will benefit from ensuring they are 'signing up' to the same deal. Share what the aims are, so that you have a shared understanding and so you all start on the 'same page'. Specifically, that this is not simply a Bible study group, nor is it counselling, nor is it just for chat. It is also not a theological study group to explore abstract matters, such as our views on millennialism, the place of the Old Testament Law today, the future of Israel, the impact of globalisation, how to improve the church, a book we just read, etc. First and foremost the Formation groups are about intentional discipleship – exploring how we are as disciples and encouraging and equipping each other in how we can grow more like Jesus, through the Word, prayer and mutual openness on some key areas of life. It is to be transforming disciples.

Committing to one another

A Formation group is initially a commitment to 6 sessions at least once a month, which might be run for 6 months. It could continue beyond that time and could involve meeting more regularly if a group wished to and that was feasible. Experience suggests they do continue beyond this point. Most groups include some purely social times too. Whichever pattern of meeting a group chooses, from the start there needs to be that commitment to one another to make the group work and give time for one another. If individuals are going to get out of the group what they hope for and also play an influential part in encouraging others, that will only happen if everyone is resolved to make time for the group and safeguard the diary dates once they are agreed. Emergencies will crop up, illnesses happen, but being a group entails a commitment to other people. This needs to be clear from the start and may need gracious reinforcement at times!

Pastoral care

These are not counselling groups. They are simply Christians getting together to grow and intentionally encourage one another in discipleship. If complex or significant pastoral issues arise, as with existing small groups, leaders may feel they wish to contact one of the pastoral leadership team. This should be the case anyway, but at times it may be helpful to encourage group members to receive further pastoral support.

It may also helpful to have a co-ordinator, which may be the minister or pastor, who keeps track of who has joined which Formation group, and roughly where each group has reached in the six-month plan, as well as providing a contact point for ongoing pastoral care support.

There is a real value in pastoral support for and from one another in the group too. To that end, regular contact between meetings is bound to be beneficial, either electronically (texts, emails, a private facebook group) or meeting over a pizza, a pint or a Saturday morning coffee.

Trust and confidentiality

As a good general rule, what is said in the group stays in the group, unless someone clearly says it can be shared. But best to assume confidentiality in all things of significance. Highlighting this will also help the group grow in confidence to open up to each other.

Listening and talking

The leaders will already be more familiar with the aims and ideas for the group before the first time they meet. They will have a sense of the structure of the evening, the Bible study material, the discipleship topic and so on. It will be helpful to send material to the group members in advance of each meeting, to prepare and look through. But inevitably the group will look to the leader to lead, so the leader needs to be mindful not to talk too much, especially early on. A group needs to encourage mutual involvement. Some people will need encouragement to talk more, and some encouragement to listen more. Perhaps taking it in turns to prepare and lead each session will be appropriate and helpful for some groups.

Prayer

Many remain lacking in confidence in praying aloud, but it's so helpful and natural. Hopefully, by virtue of being such a small group, this enables that confidence to grow. It may be good from the start to ask each person for just three things for prayer each time: a personal concern, a prayer for their family or a significant relationship, and an explicit hope for spiritual growth or change. Texting or emailing one another between meetings with prayer requests, updates and encouragement is also simple and effective. Prayer is powerful and effective, and so valuable in our growth together.

Friendship

These groups are not purely for social time or developing friendship, but this is also an important part of them, so groups should feel free on occasions to be creative and inclusive. For example, they could leave the study and questions for a week and perhaps just go out to a café, for a meal, include spouses and family as appropriate, even get the board games out.

Staying on track

There can be value in choosing as a group to devote a session to a topic that you have all found challenging as disciples, e.g. personal evangelism, relating to people of another faith, engaging biblically with a contemporary issue in society. These *can* be helpful, but the leader and group need to agree that this will be an occasional diversion, with a mutual decision to keep intentional discipleship as the main aim. Theological discussions of secondary matters of doctrine or politics from a Christian perspective may be fascinating indeed, so might football or parenting stories, but sometimes we need to put them to one side, for another time and place, when we've made the effort to create space for building each other up in Christ.

Feedback

From time to time, once a few groups are up and running, it may be helpful to gather the leaders together to share how the groups are developing. Without breaking any confidentiality, it helps to share how the materials are being used, how or when each group has arranged its meetings, particular topics that have proven engaging and fruitful, practical ideas for keeping in touch as a group, and ideas for further steps. This also raises awareness of where further input may be needed with direction or support.

Chapter 4

Bible study questions: Philippians

Formation groups exist to encourage and enable us as disciples together. They lead to transformation, to growth together and in Christ. There is no more powerful way to see this in action than engaging together with God's word, so these Bible studies are written to provide material for a 30-40 minute Bible study as a group, aiming to help deepen our understanding, to prompt reflection and to encourage personal application.

Therefore encourage one another and build each other up, just as in fact you are doing.

1 Thessalonians 5:11

Philippians

The short letter of Paul to the Christians of Philippi is passionate, personal and deeply pastoral. It gives a joyful dose of encouragement to live the Christian life, with practical wisdom too, all rooted in a clear view of Christ. Paul has been transformed by seeing Christ at work and enjoying him. Being in prison only seems to sharpen his vision and deepen that appreciation. His great joy overflows through the letter as he prays for and exhorts the church to shape their lives around Christ Jesus.

This letter has some of the most well-known words of the whole New Testament. Philippians gives us the 'hymn' to Christ who took on the nature of a man, a slave, and was obedient to death, even death on a cross, then exalted, glorified to the highest place where we confess him now as Lord of all. Paul tells us everything else is 'rubbish' (in our polite translations) compared to knowing the fullness of Christ. We are told here to keep our eyes on 'the prize', to press on to the goal. To the Philippians, Paul speaks of Christ our peace, 'which transcends all understanding', guarding our hearts and minds, and an antidote to anxiety.

This letter has been medicine for the soul, food for the spiritually hungry, a means of grace to the church for over 2000 years, and it still speaks to us today. In particular, it offers a view and encounter with Christ that is practical, powerful and personal – as Paul had found. May we seek that too.

These six studies consider the whole of the letter, seeking to deepen understanding and offer prompts for application. Take time before each session to read the text, praying for God to speak, noting questions, and preparing to encourage one another as you open up scripture together.

We have encouraged groups to start with the Philippians studies as they are relatively short, it is a short letter in itself, it is familiar to many Christians, and it has a clear focus on the gospel and on Christ. It is a letter full of joy!

Your word is a lamp for my feet, a light on my path.

Psalm 119:105

Session 1

Philippians 1:1-11

> *... he who began a good work in you will carry it on to completion until the day of Christ Jesus.*
> **Philippians 1:6**

What do you thank God for most 'deeply' in your prayers? (**v.3**)

Paul's abundant joy comes from reflecting on and sharing in a 'partnership in the gospel' (**v.5**) with others. How do we see our connection with Jesus and with his people? How is it a blessing to us?

How do we understand the 'good work' which God began in us? (**v.6**) Having begun it, how do we expect God's help and presence to 'complete' it?

(**vv.9-11**) What would be your hopes and prayers for your Christian growth – in this group, over the next few months? How would you apply vv.9-11 to your hopes?

End this session with prayer for each other.

Session 2

Philippians 1:12-29

> *... I eagerly expect and hope that I will in no way be ashamed, but will have sufficient courage so that now as always Christ will be exalted in my body, whether by life or by death.*
> **Philippians 1:20**

How do you relate to Paul's sense of confidence and even boldness in being a Christian (**vv.12-15**)?

Paul has confidence in Christ even when circumstances are difficult, rejoicing in Christ (**v.16, 30**, also **2:17** - Paul in chains). Have we experienced this? How can we grow in expectation?

Paul 'eagerly expects' God's welcome, affirmation, rescue, new life. What is his attitude to life and death (**v.20**)?

(**v.27**) 'Conduct yourselves in a manner worthy of the gospel of Christ'. 'stand firm ... believe ... suffer ... struggle'. How does such a life look distinctive, different, compared to the world's values? How can we live like this?

End this session with prayer for each other.

Session 3

Philippians 2:1-18

> *... continue to work out your salvation with fear and trembling, for it is God who works in you to will and to act in order to fulfill his good purpose.* **Philippians 2:12-13**

Notice the sense of unity with other Christians (**vv.1-2**) – 'united with Christ', 'fellowship with the Spirit', 'one in spirit and purpose'. In which relationships or context do you rejoice in this sense of unity? How are you encouraged? Where are you contributing to this?

The example and role of Jesus is so clear (**vv.5-11**) – his humility, his selfless sacrifice, his greatness and honour in God's eyes despite the shame in the world's eyes, his glory and authority at the judgement. How do these speak to us today?

(**vv.12-13**) We are to 'work out our salvation', while 'God works in you'. How can we be more intentional to let Him work in us?

(**vv.17-18**) Where are you encouraged by the witness, service, example or inspiration of other Christians you know?

End this session with prayer for each other.

Session 4

Philippians 2:19-30

> *I have no one else like him, who will show genuine concern for your welfare. For everyone looks out for their own interests, not those of Jesus Christ.* **Philippians 2:20-21**

(**v.19**) How does Christian friendship keep you going and growing as a Christian?

(**v.21**) What does it mean to 'look out for the interests of Christ Jesus' in the spiritual welfare of others? How can we do that, in practical terms?

How can we minister to other Christian friends? What stops us or holds us back from being more open or more involved in talking of spiritual matters?

Take a moment to share and give thanks for those who have been a ‘Timothy’ or an ‘Epaphroditus’ for you (**v.25**), a ‘brother or sister, co-worker, fellow soldier, a messenger of the good news’, used by the Lord to bless you.

End this session with prayer for each other.

Session 5

Philippians 3:1 – 4:1

> *... I consider everything a loss because of the surpassing worth of knowing Christ Jesus my Lord, for whose sake I have lost all things. ... I want to know Christ* **Philippians 3:8,10**

(**vv.7-8**) Paul is consumed with knowing Christ, and considers all else 'rubbish' by comparison. Discuss! What has been the best thing this past month about knowing Christ? How might we have we under-valued Christ, or over-valued other things?

(**v.9**) We belong to Christ - accepted, loved, and righteous – by faith in Christ. This righteousness is a gift, not based on our performance. How does this put our failings into perspective? How can this make us more confident Christians?

(**vv.13-14**) We are on a journey, in a race, in a fight, to reach the goal, to win the prize. How can we be encouraged by the example of Jesus (e.g. **Phil. 2:5-11**)? What other, lesser 'prize' might we strive to win?

(**vv.16-17**) How can we encourage one another to more godly living, as citizens of heaven (**v.20**) whilst living on earth?

End this session with prayer for each other.

Session 6

Philippians 4:2-23

> *Rejoice in the Lord always. I will say it again: Rejoice! Let your gentleness be evident to all. The Lord is near.* **Philippians 4:4-5**

Every Christian has their name in the 'book of life', yet they don't always behave well or get on together. How do you personally cope with conflict with Christians?

'Rejoice ... The Lord is near.' (**vv.4-5**) Are there times when you have particularly needed to know or wanted to know that 'the Lord is near'?

(**v.7**) God's peace (both from God, and the peace that only He gives) guards our hearts and minds in Christ Jesus, as we take matters to Him in prayer, as we open ourselves to His nearness and presence, and move from anxiety to trust. How have you experienced this? Why do we get anxious at times?

Our minds are easily distracted, even polluted, hence Paul's command (**vv.8-9**). How can we enable ourselves, and encourage others, to seek this renewed thinking?

The Philippians were generous to Paul, to one another and to the needy in financial support and in other ways. How should we apply this to ourselves, in general and in practical ways?

End this session with prayer for each other.

Chapter 5

Bible study questions: Psalms

Formation groups exist to encourage and enable us as disciples together. They lead to transformation, to growth together and in Christ. There is no more powerful way to see this in action than engaging together with God's word, so these Bible studies are written to provide material for a 40-50 minute Bible study as a group, aiming to help deepen our understanding, to prompt reflection and to encourage personal application.

Therefore encourage one another and build each other up, just as in fact you are doing.

1 Thessalonians 5:11

The Psalms

The book of Psalms includes some of the most well-known words in all of the Bible. It also includes some of the most heart-felt cries, prayers of longing and of loss alongside joy and triumph; we can find anguished complaint, bold confidence, urgent petition, deep trust. Wherever we find ourselves in terms of our experience of faith in God, our walk with Christ and human life in general, Psalms has words for us. It captures the length and breadth of human experience from a believer's standpoint. So it is a rich treasure trove for us as disciples today.

It can provide comfort and reassurance, challenge and encouragement, and force us to a deeper honesty before God. The Psalms give us vocabulary for our prayer and praise. There is perhaps no book like it in the Bible for refreshing the weary, restoring our vision and simply giving us words to take back to God.

These six Psalms in the studies that follow provide just a sample. They offer a variety of prayers and themes. They seek to deepen understanding and offer prompts for application. Take time before each session to read the text, praying for God to speak, noting questions, and preparing to encourage one another as you open up scripture together.

Your word is a lamp for my feet, a light on my path.

Psalm 119:105

Session 1

Psalm 1 *A fruitful life*

The activities of 'walking', 'standing' and 'sitting' in **verse 1** suggest someone increasingly comfortable and settled, fitting in with 'wicked, sinners, mockers'. They are conforming and joining in with their values, their perspective, their attitude to God and his ways. Following this path there is no prospect of enjoying God's blessing or life.

- What could this look like?
- Where and how are we influenced?
- Some choose to sideline God, others drift. What can cause this?
- How can we guard ourselves from being influenced in ways that lead us astray and away from the Lord?

The alternative life is depicted as that of drawing deeply on God's directions and ways, firstly speaking of his words (**verse 2**).

- How can we 'get into' the Bible more deeply and regularly, and let it 'get into' us more? What hinders this for us?

Verse 3 depicts a fruitful, living, growing, abundant tree.

- How would you relate this to a Christian's life?

- God's aim for us is not 'health, wealth and happiness', so what are the signs of the 'good life' that Psalm 1 symbolises?

The way without God leads to ruin (literally, a road that disappears; a sense of lacking substance or hope; a pointless path).

By contrast, **verse 6**

- What does this convey of God's care and character? How do you respond to this?

Give thanks for signs of fruitful growth in your life, and consider where God wants to bring refreshment, drawing deep on him, perhaps where new growth needs to begin.

End this session with prayer for each other.

Session 2

Psalm 19 *Enjoying God's world and his word*

(**vv.1-4**) When did you last enjoy something of God's good creation?

- How did it affect you, 'speak' to you the true words of God without audible speech (**v.3**)?

Creation exists in part to display the glory of God and to nourish our souls. It is capable of expanding our senses, to experience and enjoy beauty, wonder and awe, all of which we also find in our Creator.

- How could you create fresh opportunities to enjoy beauty, and experience wonder and awe?

(**vv.7-9**) God's written word also 'refreshes the soul', it brings wisdom and joy, and helps us see ahead.

- How have we seen these in our lives?

- When do we allow ourselves simply to listen and receive His words? How can we give our soul that regular refreshment?

(**v.10**) God's word is a treasure, a sweet nourishment, a protection, a prize.

- How do we make use of it to know these blessings? What do we do in practical terms to bring God's word to our mind and heart?

(**vv.13-14**) These words, when heard and applied, guard and nurture our soul, enable a right heart towards God (in speech and thought).

- How would you express this work that God does to bring us closer to him ... Our Rock and our Redeemer? How has he changed you?

End this session with prayer for each other.

Session 3

Psalm 20 *God in our hurting*

So many of the psalms give clear expression of deep cries of the heart to God. (**v.1**)

- Do you find you can relate to this? How?

(**v.2**) A prayer for 'help' and 'support' in our distress. God does not promise to remove or solve difficulties necessarily. He can, sometimes he does, often he doesn't. But he does promise his presence in our distress and difficulty, his faithful kindness, his strength to lean on.

- How have you experienced this?
- What does it tell us about the Lord?

(**v.4**) It is certainly not wrong to pray for our 'heart's desires', and to continue 'making plans'.

- How do we balance this with 'Your will be done'?
- Are we open to God setting plans for us that are inconvenient or costly, running against our plans?

Yet it's still ok to be honest with our desires, and proactive in planning.

(v.7)

- What are the 21st Century equivalents of 'horses and chariots', that we might be tempted to trust in?

When we say we trust in the 'name' of the Lord, that isn't literally just his name, a title, a verbal declaration that we trust God. His 'Name' is all that he is in reputation, honour, nature and power. It encompasses all his promises for us.

- Which promises or aspects of God's character do we particularly value, especially in our distress?

End this session with prayer for each other.

Session 4

Psalm 23 *The Lord, our Shepherd*

The idea of a 'shepherd' is quite remote for most of us. It was not remote for David, of course, who learned the hard graft of shepherding sheep and fighting wild animals before facing the giant Goliath and the hard graft of shepherding Israel. A 'shepherd' in the Old Testament is often far more than someone looking after sheep; it conveys the idea of a ruler, leader, king (e.g. Numbers 27:17; Ezekiel 34:2-3; 1 Chronicles 17:6; Jeremiah 23:4; Psalm 78:72). Jesus is the ultimate Good Shepherd (John 10:11; 1 Peter 5:4).

So this Psalm conveys a sense of the LORD's rule, his leadership, his care and protection, and his provision for the sheep.

- How does it help you to reflect on the LORD as <u>*your*</u> shepherd?

David emphasizes that with the LORD as his shepherd, he lacks nothing.

- How would you describe what he receives (**vv.2-6**), so he can says he lacks no good thing?
- How have you received these things?

- Have you known a dark valley experience? If so, how did you know God's help there?

We might consider our need of spiritual and physical care, of direction, of spiritual security and assurance, of moral correction, of hope, or protection.

- Why do we need these things?

The shepherd's 'rod and staff' indicate his very real authority over us (sheep obey the shepherd), and also his careful discipline (sheep are brought back when straying). We value the care of the shepherd, but perhaps resist his discipline and direction.

- How do we experience the 'rod and the staff' in our lives with Christ? Are we alert to what he wants?

v.6 What does it mean that God's 'goodness and love' will 'follow me' to life's end?

- How does Jesus, the good shepherd, fulfil this psalm for us?

End this session with prayer for each other.

Session 5

Psalm 51 *Confession, restoration and renewal*

Sin, wrongdoing, transgression, iniquity. We don't want to think about this, and understandably so. But one reason we struggle with forgiveness of others is we have not taken to heart forgiveness for ourselves, and realized how deep, powerful and cleansing God's grace is. To truly understand that amazing grace, we also need a view of how deep, real and dark is sin, which Psalm 51 conveys very clearly. It also speaks of what God offers in response to our heartfelt confession. So it's not so much about us simply being sinful, but also how God relates to us as sinners.

This Psalm comes from a very dark, painful place in the life of David, after he had demonstrated lust, covetousness, deceit, adultery and murder. We are not in that same place, but the Psalm opens up the nature of sin. But there is amazing grace for us too. The psalm paints a wonderful picture of how our confession is followed by God's restoration and renewal.

The psalmist cries out for mercy and is confident in God's love not failing (**v.1**). This view of God has a clear view of his holiness, and holds on to his love too.

He uses three different words for sin: transgressions (losing our way, straying from the right path, crossing moral boundaries), iniquity (being unclean, a stain, moral guilt or being dirty), and sin (morally falling short, wrongdoing).

- What does it tell us that there are so many ways used to describe sin in Psalm 51?
- How can we stop to examine ourselves, our hearts?
- How do we relate to God when we sense our wrongdoing, failure or sinful ways?

There is no avoiding the fact that we sin, fail, fall short, as the psalm acknowledges (**vv.3-6**). And God clearly offers cleansing, forgiveness, a barrier removed, restoration. Reflect on **vv.10-12**.

> 10 *Create in me a pure heart, O God, and renew a steadfast spirit within me. ...* 12 *Restore to me the joy of your salvation and grant me a willing spirit, to sustain me.*

- How does God work to do this? How have you experienced it?
- How do you find your joy in God?
- Why would we pray for a 'steadfast' and 'willing' spirit?

The psalmist will speak of God and sing of God having renewed him, telling and teaching others of how good God is (**vv.13-15**). A renewed life spills out; it can't and won't be hidden.

The psalm ends with a very tender picture of how God views us in our honesty and brokenness, where he meets us to restore, forgive, cleanse and rebuild, **vv.16-17**

> *[16] You do not delight in sacrifice, or I would bring it; you do not take pleasure in burnt offerings. [17] The sacrifices of God are a broken spirit; a broken and contrite heart, O God, you will not despise.*

Our world tells us to 'be strong', 'be true to yourself', and generally looks down on signs of weakness, humility, failure. God tells us he is strong, be true to him, and come with our weakness.

- How can we develop a healthy vulnerability with God?

- How can we develop a healthy vulnerability with other people close to us?

End this session with prayer for each other.

Session 6

Psalm 91 *Resting in God's shadow*

Many of the psalms use pictures, metaphors, to depict our relationship to the Lord. They put into vivid imagery how we relate to him, what we receive from him, and the world we live in.

Psalm 91 focuses on our security and assurance in God, a theme which runs deeply through the whole of the Bible, not least because people in every generation struggle with this and may feel they lack such security. Others simply take it for granted, which may also be unhelpful. The writer gives us reasons for clear certainty and prompts us to avoid complacency.

> ***vv.1-2*** *He who dwells in the shelter of the Most High will rest in the shadow of the Almighty.* [2] *I will say of the LORD, "He is my refuge and my fortress, my God, in whom I trust."*

It conveys a sense of complete security, unthreatened and absolute. It begins with rest. Not with effort, activity or achievement.

Try being quiet and still before God. Take a few moments to reflect on being at rest in his shadow, his presence.

- What is this 'rest' for you? How can we practice it?
- How do we rest from spiritual striving, not just physical busyness?

To rest in God's 'shadow' is an image of closeness, intimacy with God. Near enough to be in his shadow.

- How do you benefit from knowing that God promises such closeness, even if at times he feels absent or distant?

Verse 2 feels like an oath, a resolution being made. Resolving to know God as a 'refuge and fortress' – a place to retreat to, strong and secure, defended against all attacks.

- What attacks our sense of assurance, our spiritual vitality or wellbeing?

- How does this Psalm provide help for us?

The Psalm continues (**vv.3-13**) by declaring the reality of God's protection and security, that we need have no fear, despite troubles or dangers, natural or supernatural, real or imaginary. This isn't a literal antidote to all harm in a fallen world; just reading most of the Psalms tells us that. It is a promise that nothing happens outside of God's care and presence with us. Nothing.

- How does God's presence, the reality of God with us, change our perspective on worry (potential troubles)?

- How do his shelter and care change how we face actual troubles?

> **vv.14-16** *"Because he loves me," says the LORD, "I will rescue him; I will protect him, for he acknowledges my name. [15] He will call upon me, and I will answer him; I will be with him in trouble, I will deliver him and honor him. [16] With long life will I satisfy him and show him my salvation.*

To 'love' God is to deeply desire the Lord, to pay close attention to him and his ways. God rewards this 'love', this 'acknowledgement' with answered prayers, reassurance and peace (**v.15**), with forgiveness and joy, and with the certainty of eternal life (**v.16**).

End this session with prayer for each other.

Chapter 6

Bible study questions: John's Gospel, chs. 13-16

Formation groups exist to encourage and enable us as disciples together. They lead to transformation, to growth together and in Christ. There is no more powerful way to see this in action than engaging together with God's word, so these Bible studies are written to provide material for a 40-50 minute Bible study as a group, aiming to help deepen our understanding, to prompt reflection and to encourage personal application.

Therefore encourage one another and build each other up,
just as in fact you are doing.

1 Thessalonians 5:11

John's Gospel, chapters 13-16

The middle section of John's Gospel has immense dramatic power. The drama of chapters 13-16 is concentrated in one room, amidst a close-knit group of friends, including a series of shocking events and turns of conversation, from foot-washing to betrayal, all centred on Jesus. The Lord and his disciples are in the upper room. It is the night before his death and Jesus prepares his disciples for life beyond this point. It is an extraordinary evening, with life-changing prospects and promises far beyond the horizon of even those historic few days.

Jesus says quite clearly that he will be leaving them yet he will be with them. These chapters take us into that room, listening and watching, to find God's words also to us about the very heart of knowing and trusting Jesus. The work and ministry of the Holy Spirit are prominently highlighted by the Lord, showing us what to expect of this life as disciples. It is a call to a life following Jesus, intimately dependent on him, assured of his love, experiencing growth, yet also knowing trials and hardship. It gives us an intimate picture of Jesus and his friends, and invites us to experience that and understand more of this intimate life with him and his Spirit.

These six studies take us to Jesus. They encourage and challenge us to listen to him and apply his message, promises and challenges to ourselves. The studies seek to deepen our understanding and offer prompts for application. Take time before each session to read the text, praying for God to speak, noting questions, and preparing to encourage one another as you open up scripture together.

Your word is a lamp for my feet, a light on my path.

Psalm 119:105

Session 1

John 13:1-17 Our Servant King

They are gathered for a meal, but little is said of the meal itself over these chapters. There is no mention anywhere in John's Gospel of the Lord's supper, breaking bread or wine as symbols of his death, no eucharist, no communion meal, here or elsewhere. Because John is concerned throughout that we see that ***we are saved through Jesus and him alone***. He clears the way for us to see Jesus. It's not that the meal didn't happen; this chapter mentions 'the meal' but doesn't dwell on it. We know from Matthew, Mark and Luke's accounts that Jesus interpreted the bread or wine to point to his saving death, but we should see what *John* wants us to see – only Jesus offers new life. No sacrament or religious activity can replace or add to Jesus.

This Jesus lived, died, rose again and ascended for us, not to leave us a sacrament in itself, but to leave us - in John's words - the blessing of eternal life, joy complete, the bread of life, true light in our darkness.

Read John 13:1-17

Around this meal table, the main activity in this episode is not eating but foot-washing. v.1 links this evening, and Jesus' actions, to the Passover festival, the events of God's rescue and mercy, deliverance from wrath and from death. His footwashing links to his forthcoming death as the new Passover Lamb:

> ***v.1** the hour had come … Having loved his own who were in the world, he now showed them the full extent of his love.*

There is a **particular love of God** in Christ for 'his own', distinct and qualitatively different to God's love for 'the world', for Christians now belong in Christ. Over the next few hours and days the disciples in this room would witness the extent of Jesus' love for them.

- How does it encourage you to be one of 'his own'? Consider what he did for you in his sacrifice, self-giving, suffering and death, out of love for you.

The footwashing is symbolic of **the spiritual cleaning from Jesus**. As they are washed on the outside, so he would wash them completely.

- What do you understand by Jesus' cleansing of your soul?

- As the disciples learned, they needed to let Jesus do this, let him serve them and clean them. How do we resist Jesus still?

Peter was resistant to being washed, being served by Jesus. Out of shame, the indignity of it or pride he would have none of it. Yet Jesus gently insisted and persisted. We are fully forgiven in Christ once we repent and believe, turning wholeheartedly from sin to depend on our Saviour and follow him. But we will still sin, fall short and fail. The power of sin still influences us, even if we are holy and new in God's eyes.

- Do we recognize our ongoing need to go back to God and receive assurance of forgiveness? What hinders our regular or honest confession to Him?

The humility of Jesus is striking. Jesus assumed the role and status of the lowest slave of the household. Washing feet was seen as grim and shameful work, even amongst slaves. Yet Jesus was about to go 'lower' still (Philippians 2:5-8, 'even to death, to death on a cross'). To wash feet, to bear sin, was to set aside honour and status and himself in order to serve.

- What do we learn here from Jesus of the call to serve others?
- How does the humility of Jesus shape our Christian life, our choices and our priorities?

> **John 13:15-17** *I have set you an example that you should do as I have done for you. I tell you the truth, no servant is greater than his master, nor is a messenger greater than the one who sent him. Now that you know these things, you will be blessed if you do them.*

End this session with prayer for each other.

Session 2

John 13:18-38 Rejection and Glory

Read John 13:18-38

Acceptance (vv.18-21)

Firstly, Jesus speaks of those who accept him, and in doing so they accept 'the one who sent me' (John 13:20). Jesus has been sent by the Father, the Lord God Himself. This close connection between Father and Son, and Jesus as the 'sent one', is prominent throughout John's gospel (e.g. John 3:16; 5:24, 37; 12:44-45, 49). To know Jesus is to know the Father, to know God Himself.

- Accepting Jesus brings us at one and the same time into the glorious new identity of being children of God (John 1:12). We have that security, love and protection from our heavenly Father. How do you relate to this or understand this? How does it affect you?

Rejection (vv.21-30)

Jesus knows that Judas is plotting to betray him. They share in a situation of great intimacy of a celebratory meal (even the Passover, a holy and joyful occasion). They are amongst close friends, in a private group, and with Jesus actually serving food to Judas. Jesus loves even Judas to the end.

Judas is given a clear final opportunity to love and to trust, or to reject and betray. Jesus makes a final appeal to his friend's conscience.

- What does this say of the character of Jesus, his love towards 'lost sheep'?
- How have you experienced God's appeal to your conscience?
- Perhaps you have experienced betrayal, a friend letting you down badly. How does the experience of Jesus impact you?

Evil was at work, yet it was the decision of Judas to betray Jesus. Of course, in the end all his friends would flee and desert Jesus, even deny him publicly. Yet God's purpose was not thwarted.

Glory (vv.31-38)

Jesus is heading for glory – his glorious heavenly throne, and before that the cross and gloriously new resurrection life. However, in his view at this point is the cross where he will be 'lifted up' (John 3:14-15; 8:28; 12:32) and bring new life to all who believe in him.

- Jesus saw the cross as a time and place of glory. Read Galatians 6:14 and 1 Corinthians 2:2. Are you confident in his cross, in his glorious achievement for you?

Jesus commands his disciples to love one another (v.34). He declares that love is the evidence of our discipleship. But this love is only possible when we are connected (you can't love someone you never meet), and Jesus frequently emphasises our discipleship, our life ***together***. The church is the body of Christ, a small group or Formation group can't replace the church where the body is fed and cared for, worships, grows, serves, ministers, builds, encourages and belongs together.

- How can we encourage one another to be more deeply connected to one another in the church?
- How can we help those who are having 'out of body experiences' (i.e. those who attend rarely, commit minimally, or are not opening up their the lives to the encouragement or input of others)?
- How can we serve one another?

End this session with prayer for each other.

Session 3

John 14:1-7 The only way is Christ

Read John 14:1-7

In the face of his own betrayal and impending suffering, humiliation and death, Jesus shows sincere concern for his friends. Even now his love for others is clear and paramount. He appears still to be fully trusting in his heavenly Father, and calls them to trust rather than be overcome with fear.

> **John 14:1** *Do not let your hearts be troubled. Trust in God; trust also in me.*

- In the context of this meal, this night, and Jesus' impending departure (13:33,36) what would they be troubled by?
- When are our hearts 'troubled'?
- Why is trust the antidote to troubled hearts?

> **John 14:2** *In my Father's house are many rooms; if it were not so, I would have told you. I am going there to prepare a place for you.*

Jesus speaks of his Father's welcome and home, the eternal dwelling place of God, with a sense of its spacious provision for all whom Jesus invites. Jesus goes ahead of them, the

Son of the Father, which in this culture was like one preparing a future home for extended family to join the household, to share the family home.

- In Christ, our eternal hope is to live with God, in the new heaven and new earth, recreated and renewed (Isaiah 65:17; 2 Peter 3:13; Rev. 21:1-3). How does this shape how you live now? How does it help when your heart is 'troubled'?

Jesus is ready and waiting for us (v.3)!

In answering his disciples and their confusion as to 'what are you talking about, where are you going?', and Thomas's question about the way, Jesus makes this singular and striking declaration:

> **John 14:6** *I am the way and the truth and the life. No one comes to the Father except through me.*

Each of these is intentionally exclusive: not a way, or one of many valid ways, but *the* way. The only way. The only ultimate truth or reality. The only source of life; full and eternal life with God. He is emphatically, controversially clear.

- What does it mean for us to accept and trust Jesus as 'the way', the authoritative direction and calling over our lives?

- Surrounded by the views of the prevailing world from the news, film, books, celebrity culture, friends and family, 'truth' is easily defined as 'what most people believe'. What does it mean to identify truth with Jesus himself? How do we keep in line with him?

- He came to bring life, and life in all its fullness (John 10:10). What brings us most joy in our life with Christ? Where are we prone to being distracted from him, as if life is ultimately found elsewhere?

End this session with prayer for each other.

Session 4

John 14:8-21 Never alone

The heart of our Christian experience is, quite simply, knowing God. Everything else flows from this and depends on this. In the upper room conversation, Jesus focuses on this and approaches it by talking of his own role, the love and purposes of the Father, and the activity and presence of the Holy Spirit. Each Person of the Trinity is at work in our experience of and life with God. These few chapters in John bring us to the central, deep realities of what Jesus means by 'knowing God'. In John 14:8-21, our Lord speaks of knowing the Father and the Spirit.

Read John 14:8-21

> **John 14:9-10** *Don't you know me, Philip, even after I have been among you such a long time? Anyone who has seen me has seen the Father. How can you say, 'Show us the Father'? Don't you believe that I am in the Father, and that the Father is in me?*

- How do we see the Father in and through Jesus? How was that demonstrated in Jesus' life? (see also John 1:14, 18)
- How does this shape our understanding of knowing our heavenly Father?

> **John 14:10** *The words I say to you are not just my own. Rather, it is the Father, living in me, who is doing his work.*

The *words* of Jesus are also doing the *work* of the Father – revealing God, inviting people to enter the kingdom, illuminating reality, proclaiming salvation, calling for repentance and faith, inviting a response. All of scripture is God's word, not just the recorded words of Jesus, but those words also clearly convey the Father's will for us.

- Consider the challenge of Jesus' message: where has it impacted you recently?
- Consider the promises and assurance of Jesus' message: where has it encouraged you recently?

> **John 14:15-17** *If you love me, keep my commands. And I will ask the Father, and he will give you another advocate to help you and be with you forever—the Spirit of truth.*

All three Persons of the Holy Trinity work together for the good of those who come to a saving faith. As we acknowledge our need of forgiveness by God and trust Him, by grace we receive so much. We become children of God, part of his family. The Spirit of God saves us by applying the power of what Jesus has done to our lives, uniting us to Jesus and his new life, granting us this life of Jesus and making his home in our lives, working to change us from within, empowering us to live like Christ and for Christ.

- How have you known the help or conviction of the Holy Spirit?
- How can we become more consciously dependent on the Holy Spirit?
- He is the 'Spirit of truth' – the Spirit and the Bible speak as one, never divided. How can we find practical ways to let his words shape our hearts and minds more fully?

John 14:17 *Jesus said: '**you know him**, for he lives with you and will be in you.'*

May this give you great security in your soul.

End this session with prayer for each other.

Session 5

John 15:1-17 Fruitful lives

Read John 15:1-17

It is John's Gospel that records the 'I am' statements by Jesus, the self-revelation of God in Christ (John 6:35; 8:12; 10:7, 11; 11:25; 14:6 and 15:1). They echo the words of the Lord God to Moses from within the burning bush, as our God is revealed as the great 'I AM' (Exodus 3:14). When Jesus declares, 'I am the true vine' here in chapter 15, he indicates his divine identity and calling. In the Old Testament, Israel – the people of God – were the Lord's vine (e.g. Isaiah 5:7), to be nurtured and tended by the Gardener Himself. Now Jesus declares that **he** is the centre and source of life for all God's people; we are to find our spiritual life and flourishing, individually and collectively, in relationship to Jesus. Without him, we can do nothing; spiritually we wither and die. In him, we can grow, find joy, be fruitful. And again it assumes we are joined in him together – the branches share the vine.

> **John 15:1-2** *I am the true vine, and my Father is the gardener. He cuts off every branch in me that bears no fruit, while every branch that does bear fruit he prunes so that it will be even more fruitful.*

- Jesus emphasizes that he is the true and only source of life from God, the 'true' vine. Other sources are false, empty, deceptive (Colossians 2:8). Where else do people seek spiritual fulfillment, hope or meaning?
- How did you make a conscious choice to follow Jesus, to find spiritual life in him?

God the Father is 'the gardener'. He nurtures us, brings growth (1 Corinthians 3:6-7) and prunes. He plans our days, determines our path, and disciplines us as his children.

- How have you experienced the Lord pruning and bringing growth in your life? How do you react to what Jesus says here?

> **John 15:4** *Remain in me, and I will remain in you. No branch can bear fruit by itself; it must remain in the vine.*

The imperative and encouragement of Jesus are clear: stay with me! Keep 'in me'! To his disciples who are about to flee, face persecution, be scattered and no longer have the physical presence of Jesus with them, he has already assured them of his ongoing presence by the Spirit. Now he assures them of ongoing spiritual fruitfulness 'in him'.

- What might the 'fruit' of a life in Christ look like? How can we remain intimately dependent on Jesus?

John 15:8 *This is to my Father's glory, that you bear much fruit, showing yourselves to be my disciples.*

The growth is not just for our benefit or joy, but evidence of our discipleship, that we truly are in Christ. It is also to bring glory to God.

- How can your spiritual life reflect glory to your heavenly Father?

Give thanks for the gifts you value in each other and the 'fruitfulness' in Christ you have experienced, as you end this session with prayer for each other.

Session 6

John 15:18 – 16:4 Costly discipleship

Jesus makes the clear invitation to follow, and the nature of what this entails very clear indeed. This is not a call to superficial pleasure, a religious experience or cheap grace, i.e. God's 'friendship' and favour without cost. Rather, Jesus left his first disciples and all of us who follow in no doubt that to know him is a call to costly discipleship. In making a choice to follow him as Lord, other claims to ultimate priorities in our lives are relegated or will be denied. Nothing can replace him or his role in our lives, so our loyalty is to be to him as the Lord, at the centre of our lives. He's 'Lord of all or not Lord at all'.

In seeking obedience to his commands, his call to holiness and godliness, at times we will find ourselves at odds with the world's views, values and priorities. In belonging to Christ, honouring his name, we are in a spiritual battle and open to misunderstanding, disagreements, humiliation, mocking, persecution. He said so plainly and repeatedly. Yet he is worth it, and he is with us.

Read John 15:18 – 16:4

Consider how clearly Jesus outlined the reality of persecution and opposition:

v.18 *If the world hates you* [and it will]

v.19 *That is why the world hates you.*

v.20 *they will persecute you also*

> **John 15:18-19** *If the world hates you, keep in mind that it hated me first. If you belonged to the world, it would love you as its own. As it is, you do not belong to the world, but I have chosen you out of the world. That is why the world hates you.*

- Why did Jesus experience persecution and hatred during his public ministry on earth? (Consider the political, religious and spiritual powers.)

When Jesus (and John) speak of 'the world', they mean a morally lost world, the sinful society in rebellion against God and in need of rescue and reconciliation. They don't mean the planet. It's typically a reference to how *bad* the world is, not how *big* it is.

- What does it mean that we 'do not belong to this world'? How do we grow in our new identity in Christ and allegiance to him?

- Christians in the UK are in an unusual place in history and in the world in not experiencing violent hatred and hostility for our faith. How *do* we experience the opposition of 'the world'?

> **John 15:20** *If they obeyed my teaching, they will obey yours also.*

Discipleship and loyalty to Christ are always linked to obedience to his teaching (look back to John 15:7,9-10). To 'love Jesus' is not principally a feeling or religious experience, even though we can and will feel his love for us and ours for him. The words of Jesus point to how our love for him is shown in our obedience to his ways and conforming to his will in character, speech and service, through what we teach and what we do.

- Where are we experiencing personally the challenge to hold on to Christ's teaching?

> **John 15:21** *They will treat you this way because of my name, for they do not know the one who sent me. If I had not come and spoken to them, they would not be guilty of sin; but now they have no excuse for their sin.*

Rejecting Jesus is rejecting God, 'the one who sent me', says the Lord. Yet if we *know* Jesus, we know the Father, and will find joy and security with Him. Jesus also promised us another Helper:

> **15:26-27** *When the Counsellor comes, whom I will send to you from the Father, the Spirit of truth who goes out from the Father, he will testify about me. And you also must testify, for you have been with me from the beginning.*

The Spirit is sent to us (John 14:16,26; 15:26). He is the 'Counsellor' (our Advocate, our strong Defender, who speaks in our defence and enables us to stand, who gives us support, strength, encouragement and guidance). He is the Spirit of truth (v.26) – he leads us in what is true and right about God, about ourselves, about truth. He deals in reality not appearances, lies, public opinion or guesswork. He empowers us to persevere, whether in simple daily trust or in the challenges we face.

- How have you known the help of the Holy Spirit in your Christian life?
- What would you ask of the Holy Spirit to enable you to keep going and keep growing as a disciple of Jesus?

Plan to take some time over the coming month or before your next meeting to look back over these six sessions and remind yourself, as if you were sat in that upper room, of the encouragements, challenges and promises from Christ to you.

End this session with prayer for each other.

Chapter 7

Everyday discipleship

Formation groups exist to encourage and equip us as disciples together. They lead to transformation, to growth together and in Christ. A key part of the group time is to explore how each person is doing as a disciple of Christ, and to encourage each other in that.

To help with this and to look at discipleship across the range of our whole life, six different themes are explored here with some suggestions for discussion questions. When we confess 'Jesus is Lord', we are acknowledging he rules over our life. All of it. Yet we don't readily make time to carefully examine our whole life, to think on 'how am I?', with his priorities and desires in mind. These sessions prompt us to do that.

It is very unlikely that there will be sufficient time in any one session to fully explore all the questions with everyone in the group. Use these as suggestions and prompts. Be selective. Work out what is most helpful for your group members each time. Aim to focus on the topic and encourage one another in meaningful, intentional and open interaction.

The topic areas are so significant to our everyday lives, our everyday discipleship, that realistically any one of these six topics could span several sessions. It might be helpful to cover all six and, if a group continues, begin the series again several months later. There will still be plenty to discuss and explore together.

Therefore encourage one another and build each other up, just as in fact you are doing.

1 Thessalonians 5:11

Discussion starter questions

The suggested aim for each evening, alongside Bible study and prayer time, includes 40 minutes or so for discussion around a topic with sharing and encouragement. A group can always come back to the same session topic in the future. If one particular aspect of the evening's topic stimulates meaningful discussion and is prompting good engagement with one another then the questions below have met their aim. These should be treated simply as suggestions and starting points; individuals will bring their own experience, testimony and insights to the group.

It will be helpful to take some time to reflect prior to meeting and review the questions on our own. For example, how have we seen God's blessings in each area? Where have we faced hurts or disappointment? Where do we face challenges? What do we hope for, with the Lord's leading and help?

Do keep in mind how to support one another in prayer following these discussions.

Session 1

Spiritual life and growth

> *So then, just as you received Christ Jesus as Lord, continue to live in him, rooted and built up in him, strengthened in the faith as you were taught, and overflowing with thankfulness.* **Colossians 2:6-7**

Describe how, where and when you became a Christian. Can you identify times of significant growth or apparent lack of growth since?

What most encourages you about your current life with Jesus?

(John 15:7-11) How can you discern *his* life, fruit and joy in *your* life?

Where are you concerned or challenged in terms of your own spiritual growth?

What are your hopes from this group, in terms of helping one another go deeper as disciples and be more rooted and rejoicing in Jesus?

Session 2

Prayer

> *So I say to you: Ask and it will be given to you; seek and you will find; knock and the door will be opened to you. For everyone who asks receives; he who seeks finds; and to him who knocks, the door will be opened.* **Luke 11:9-10**

> *Do not be anxious about anything, but in everything, by prayer and petition, with thanksgiving, present your requests to God. And the peace of God, which transcends all understanding, will guard your hearts and your minds in Christ Jesus.* **Philippians 4:6-7**

Describe what you would hope your prayer life would be like.

Discuss what has worked well for you – now or in the past – to enable a richer, fuller prayer life.

Are there particular barriers to prayer – of belief, or discipline, or routine?

Prayer is a response to God, an opening of the soul, an attending to Him, an admission of humility before a great and loving Father, welcomed there by our Saviour and friend the Lord Jesus, and our prayers enabled by the Holy Spirit Himself. ... Yet we all struggle with prayer. What will you focus on in the next month, in terms of your relationship with the Lord in prayer, to seek a richer, fuller prayer life?

Session 3

Character

Therefore, I urge you, brothers, in view of God's mercy, to offer your bodies as living sacrifices, holy and pleasing to God—this is your spiritual act of worship. Do not conform any longer to the pattern of this world, but be transformed by the renewing of your mind. **Romans 12:1-2**

Consider the fruit of the Spirit (Galatians 5:22-23). Am I growing in these? Where am I struggling or resistant?

Where can I see a battle to maintain or grow in Christ-like character? (Think what those closest to you might say!) Are there particular triggers to ungodly behaviour or thinking (e.g. when you're hungry, tired, alone, or feeling stressed)?

How well does my 'speech' reflect Christ-like character? (James 1:19-21; 3:1-12)

What have I found in scripture that has encouraged me along the way?

What do we think about or worry about most? (Philippians 4:8). How can we protect our hearts and minds, from which our character flows?

Session 4

Money, work and time

> *Whatever you do, work at it with all your heart, as working for the Lord, not for men, since you know that you will receive an inheritance from the Lord as a reward. It is the Lord Christ you are serving.* **Colossians 3:23-24**

Money, work, and time - are there any of these three which instinctively feel a challenge to talk openly about? Why?

Where are my current pressures, and how am I sharing those with God? With my spouse?

What is my attitude towards money and wealth at the moment? Am I anxious, content, or driven?

What is my attitude towards work and career at the moment? How can or should I bring a perspective of God's kingdom to these areas of my life?

How well am I stewarding my time? Am I anxious or concerned about this? Do I get enough rest?

Session 5

Relationships and family

> *From one man he made every nation of men, that they should inhabit the whole earth; and he determined the times set for them and the exact places where they should live.* **Acts 17:26**

Consider how you are building up key relationships as a Christian – in church, in marriage, with children.

What have you found most useful in practical terms to make relationships flourish, in terms of spiritual growth and spiritual friendship?

How could I encourage family life to have Christ's presence more central?

Where do you struggle with spiritual friendships or connection with others?

Consider one thing you would pray for to see God at work in your key relationships or family.

Session 6

Godly goals and service

> *... seek first his kingdom and his righteousness, and all these things will be given to you as well.*
> **Matthew 6:33**

If God could do anything IN you, what would that be?

If God could do anything THROUGH you, what would that be?

What godly goals do you have for yourself?

Are there areas of service which you feel challenged to consider, or wish to grow in?

Over the next few weeks and months, commit these things to prayer and share with your group anything you feel the Lord is saying to you, perhaps how you are progressing or some decisions you are weighing up.

Chapter 8

One church's experience

Every Christian is called to be a disciple and as part of the church we are all called to be making disciples. There is a variety of clear means which God has provided. These are instrumental to this growth and transformation, and we are to enjoy and participate in them. These include regularly gathering together under the faithful preaching of the Bible, worshipping together and praying together, sharing in the communion meal together, and encouraging one another to keep going in following Christ. Hebrews chapter 10, verses 24-25 are quite emphatic about the vital importance of gathering together around the word of God in particular – "don't stop, don't give up doing these things!"

The smaller 'gatherings' are also invaluable, whether that is a house group, a prayer triplet, a leadership team, praying with your spouse or work colleagues, a men's group, a women's group, the youth leaders prayer lunch or other variations on this theme. There is not one perfect way to shape a small group that suits all needs or matches all situations. Groups will vary, and the content may include more or less of the ingredients of Bible study, prayer, discussion or pizza. But feeding and shaping our faith around the Bible will transform our discipleship.

In our experience, Formation groups have been a very timely addition to the mix and very well received. They do not suit everyone and might not fit every church, but they are presented here in the hope that others find them helpful or inspire other similar approaches to engage in deeper discipleship together. However, some reflections on our experience may be helpful to share, to put the idea into a real-life context and to offer encouragement if you are looking to start them where you are.

This final chapter aims to share simply one church's experience in the hope that the idea might prompt renewed growth and desire in other churches. Our path to implement the groups is not the only way it could work, yet sharing our story may avoid some pitfalls and shed light on how it can be done.

Unlike many typical small groups, Formation groups are truly small in size.[2] They also the flexibility to accommodate busy social lives and messy diaries. Many have expressed

---

[2] One of the happiest 'small' group experiences of my life became a regular gathering of 25-30 people! Even when we split or multiplied we still had two not-so-small groups of 12-16 apiece. These were rich and rewarding times of good fun and fellowship and growth together, but not conducive to getting into deep discussions of discipleship or personal struggles.

deep gratitude for this initiative, as for some it has made it possible to join a small group for the very first time. Hungry and weary souls have found new support. Many have found real joy in getting alongside others in this accessible yet significant venture.

Formation groups also aim very intentionally, putting it simply, at "how are we doing as disciples?" This focus has demanded a level of openness, vulnerability and personal reflection that many have found quite challenging yet, at the same time, rewarding, refreshing and deeply encouraging. It has forged new friendships and deepened existing ones.

To put our experience into a context, as a local church we already included a range of existing small groups before we began implementing Formation groups. All of these had been running for years, even decades. We had various mid-week groups, some meeting in the evening and some in the day-time, with varying styles; most were very focused on Bible study and discussion, prayer was often included, others had a significant element of social events. Some groups included meals together in their programme. We also have a men's ministry and a women's ministry, both with vibrant activity and varied means to get alongside people.

Typically the larger groups meet monthly and focus on worship, a Bible talk or social activity and friendship to draw people into fellowship. These are the prominent elements, and they have a place as part of the life of a whole church life, but they don't tend to lead to group Bible study or a personal discussion with a discipleship focus. We also have a very active seniors ministry, welcoming 30-70 senior citizens into the church building for lunch and a talk twice a month, and reaching many more than that in other ways. There are also a number of prayer triplets, some of which have been going for many years bringing much blessing of support and encouragement.

Within all these groups, some 110-120 people had found a 'home'. Some belong to two or three groups (they're the small group 'junkies', on to a good thing). So it wasn't as if small groups had been tried and found wanting; far from it.

Yet there were still a very significant number, perhaps 60-70 members of the congregation, regularly with us on a Sunday, committed to this church, who did not have a 'home' in a small group. Formation groups were particularly aimed at these, many of whom lead busy lives with demanding jobs and commutes. For others their family circumstances make a regular mid-week group almost impossible. For some it was the size – the regular small groups were too large for their comfort zone. We recognised that everyone needs support and encouragement along the way, and also a change of approach can be a source of refreshment in itself, so Formation groups were developed and introduced.

This began by bringing together some potential group leaders, to explore and sharpen the idea and then consider who to invite. Within a few months, seven new groups had begun; by the end of the first year it was ten. Of the 41 people involved in these first ten groups (yes, one group cheated and had five members), 35 were in no other small groups. Some had never been in a small group before, despite being in the church for many years perhaps.

Putting this another way, the proportion of the regular church membership in a small group, studying the Bible and praying together, went up by over 40% through this relatively simple idea: a new, flexible, smaller group, with an intentional plan around discipleship – 'transforming disciples'. That proportion has continued to rise since. Alongside this, we have sought to continue to resource and support the other regular small groups.

As expected, the Formation groups have met irregularly: at varied intervals, in different venues, occasionally for a meal with the extended family members or just for coffee and calorific cakes. With a few bumps along the way, most of them have kept going over 12-18 months since we started and have stayed on course. It has also brought tangible encouragement, growth, joy and motivation to those involved.

Some groups have occasionally gone off the beaten track, perhaps spending a session focused on a particular Bible text of interest, or a theological topic one of the group is wrestling with, then returned to the main path of Bible study, discipleship questions and prayer.

The Bible study materials continue to be supplemented.

Groups started with the studies on Philippians, as a short and often familiar letter with a clear focus on the gospel, then moved on to the longer studies in the Psalms, John's Gospel or other materials. Similar material has been written and provided as the Bible study element of the groups remains at the core. It may be that some groups choose to use existing Bible study resources published elsewhere; as long as the aims of the group are held to and reflected in how the group spends their time, i.e. letting the Bible speak into everyday discipleship with mutual honesty and encouragement, then clearly other Bible study notes can be very helpful.

After several sessions all the initial groups decided to continue, with only one or two people stepping out of groups for personal reasons. The remainder have found it valuable and encouraging and they are looking to keep going together as relationships also deepen.

Formation groups are by no means a new or radical idea, it feels as old as the hills to do this and other churches have similar groups by other names, but they have been a very helpful, encouraging new experience in this local church family and the idea has been picked up elsewhere.

It is a sign of God's grace that he continues to work through his people, doing these quite 'ordinary' activities of sharing our lives together around the Bible, and he brings the growth and many blessings besides. Formation groups are just a part of all that we have to be grateful to God for as a local church family.

Our hope is that this book might provide others with a simple resource and a renewed encouragement to aim for transforming disciples, extending the 'fridge rights' and seeing deeper fellowship and new growth in Christ as a result.

Feedback

If you pick up this book somehow (either online or in one of those rare and wonderful places, a "bookshop") and then decide to pick up the idea itself and put it into practice, I would love to hear how it goes. Any such feedback would be appreciated.

If you have any helpful comments on the material, extra topics of everyday discipleship you found people engaged with well, experiences to share of how you implemented the groups, or what else you did to help a church engage with Formation groups ... then please drop me a line via Ampthill Baptist Church.

Thank you.

ACKNOWLEDGEMENTS

With grateful thanks to the fellowship at Ampthill Baptist Church, especially those who took hold of the Formation groups idea with enthusiasm and willingness, and have given me much encouragement since.

ABOUT THE AUTHOR

Andrew Goldsmith is married with two children and is currently serving as Senior Pastor of Ampthill Baptist Church in Bedfordshire.

He has been in ministry for over 10 years with an emphasis on Bible preaching and teaching and everyday discipleship. He also enjoys creative and lively ways to engage in apologetics (explaining and defending Christianity, trying to clear the big questions out of the way) and helping people connect with Jesus through the Bible.

He has been in leadership of churches in Leeds and NW London and studied at London School of Theology. Prior to pastoral church ministry he worked in industry and academia in the area of medical engineering, developing replacement hip and knee joints.

25545684R00061

Printed in Great Britain
by Amazon